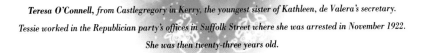

Teresa O'Connell, from Castlegregory in Kerry, the youngest sister of Kathleen, de Valera's secretary. Tessie worked in the Republician party's offices in Suffolk Street where she was arrested in November 1922. She was then twenty-three years old.

Catalana Bulfin, the daughter of William Bulfin, author of Rambles in Éirinn.
Born in Argentina, the youngest of five children, she was affectionately known as 'kid'. She worked in
Austin Stack's office, where she was arrested in 1923. The twenty-three year old Catalana was not a
member of Cumann na mBan but knew many activists. She later married Seán MacBride, who took this
photograph of her on their honeymoon in France in 1926. He was on the run at the time.

GUNS & *Chiffon*

1916-1923

© Government of Ireland 1997

ISBN 0 7076 3870 4

Dublin: Published by the Stationery Office.

To be purchased directly from the
Government Publications Sale Office.
Sun Alliance House, Molesworth Street, Dublin 2.

or by mail order from
Government Publications. Postal Trade Section.
4-5 Harcourt Road, Dublin 2.
Tel: 01-661 3111 ext. 4040/4045 Fax: 01-475 2760
or through any bookseller

Written by
Sineád McCoole

Advised by
Pat Cooke

Designed by
Creative Inputs

Separations by
Graphic Media Management

Printed by
Nicholson & Bass Ltd

Cover
Mollie Gill active in the Civil War (1922-24)
Maud Gonne founder of Inghinidhe na hÉireann (1900)

£5.00

CONTENTS

———————

A C K N O W L E D G E M E N T S

*T*his booklet would not have been possible without the guidance and editorial assistance of Pat Cooke, Manager of Kilmainham Gaol; Paul Turnell, who undertook painstaking research in London; Niamh O'Sullivan, who takes charge of the archives and was a conscientious proof reader; The staff of Kilmainham Gaol who assisted at every opportunity - Tim Carey, Supervisor and Elizabeth Carey, Brian Crowely, Sheena Maloney, Phyl Mason, Gillian Mullen, Aoife McMahon, Catherine O'Connor, William Peters and Gavan Woods. I am also grateful to Henriette Benson, Carla Briggs, Isabel Donnellan, Dr. Margaret Mac Curtain and Jim Larner, Head of Publications. Peter Monaghan and Helen Hayes for her thoughtful design. I am also indebted, as always, to my family and Eamon.

For those who provided information and photographs: Con Brady, the late Nora Brosnan, Oliver and Cheryl Brosnan, Bernard Browne, the Burke family, Maureen Cashman, Ann Claire, Anne Clarke, Dr Emmet Clarke, Seamus Connolly, Joe Craven, Margaret Cullinane, Maeve Donnelly, Celine Doyle, the late Ita Draper, Una Dunne, Peter Berresford Ellis, Anne Fagan, Sally Feore, Frances Fleming, Chris Halpin, Alan Hayes, Eleanor Hunt, Peggy Jordan, JJ Kelly, Laurie Lawless, Kate Lowe, Cróine and Manchán Magan, Anne Matthews, the late Tiernan MacBride, Christopher McCann, Anne MacDonagh, Iseult MacGuinness, Laura McGuirk, Eithne McKeown, Deirdre McKervey, Anne McMahon, Loretta and Gerald Murray, Seamus Murphy, Brother Fintan Norris, Louie O'Brien, Teresa O'Connell, Patrick Pearse O'Daly, Teresa O'Dwyer, Terry O'Flaherty, Louise O'Hánrahan, Eithne O'Moore, Marie O'Neill, Conor O'Neill, Michael Purcell, Kevin Rooney, Odran Seeley, Leo Smith, Joe Tierney, Cissie and Lily Thewliss, John Power, Margaret Ward, Dr Ann-Maree Whitaker and Anna MacBride White.

I am grateful to the staff of The British Public Record Office, Kew, (PRO); Military Archives Cathal Brugha Barracks; National Library of Ireland, in particular, Dave MacLoughlin; Ian Lee of the RTE Sound Archive, Trinity College Dublin and University College Dublin Archive, The Labour History Museum and Jean Hazlett of the Alexandra College Archive.

For granting me copyright permission, I wish to thank The Board of Trinity College Dublin; Anne Gallagher for allowing me to quote her mother Cecilia

Saunders Gallagher; The Sligo County Art Gallery and Anne Yeats for permission to use 'Communicating with Prisoners' by Jack B. Yeats, John Searle photographer; and University College Dublin Archive for allowing me to quote from the O'Brennan papers, Charlotte Fallon's thesis and the Coyle O'Donnell papers; The Trustees of the National Library of Ireland to quote from the Grace Plunkett and Bridget Lyons Thornton manuscripts and to reproduce images of Fanny and Anna Parnell, Dr. Kathleen Lynn and Madeleine ffrench-Mullen; Alexandra College for permission to use material from their archive. The Crown Copyright material in the Public Record Office, Kew is reproduced with the permission of the Controller of Her Majesty's Stationary Office.

For anyone I have omitted to mention I extend my apologies. In some cases it has not been possible to trace the holders of original copyrights, this will be amended in future editions. All the errors are the author's own.

Annie Derham née Hampton c.1916.

INTRODUCTION
Guns and Chiffon

*B*ean na hÉireann, (1908-1911) the first Irish woman's newspaper, was described by its editor Helena Molony as *'a mixture of guns and chiffon'*. This image can also serve as a metaphor for the contradictory nature of the women's role in the struggle for Irish freedom. Their involvement in revolutionary politics was seen as irreconcilable with the feminine aspects of their personalities and their role as mothers, wives and sweethearts. Indeed women's involvement in any form of political activity was regarded as an unwomanly form of behaviour. However, a woman writing in the *Irish Freedom* told her readers in 1913:

There is nothing unwomanly in active patriotism. Nobody calls Jeanne d'Arc unwomanly, nor Anne Devlin ... whatever conservative-minded people may say to you now about the unseemliness of women actively and openly working for their country's cause: yet in the days when Ireland is free, no one will have anything but admiration for the women who contributed ... [1]

The images of women dressed in the fine flimsy material of chiffon (photographs of Maud Gonne MacBride and Countess Constance Markievicz in evening dresses) are difficult to reconcile with those of women wielding guns. Yet the change in the outward appearance of women reflected a new liberation. Countess Markievicz wrote in 1915: *'dress suitably in short skirts and strong boots, leave your jewels and gold wands* (sic) *in the bank, and buy a revolver.'* [2] The coarse tweed of the Cumann na mBan uniform with its military lines was seen as suppressing femininity. Beauty was of secondary importance and even the use of make-up was viewed as unpatriotic.

Those women who opted for the revolutionary role were in the minority. Through tenacity and independence of character they broke with the behavioural norms of the time. This ensured their commitment to the cause and an unswerving attitude to ideological issues. It is striking, for example, how many of the leading republican women remained adamantly opposed to the Treaty. Over 300 women were imprisoned in Kilmainham Gaol during the Civil War.

The women involved in the struggle for Irish political independence 1916-1923 were part of the long tradition of Irish patriotism. No less than the men, they were willing to give their lives for their ideals and to endure the rigors of hunger strike and separation from friends and family for their beliefs. Young mothers in particular suffered during the long months of incarceration. However, history has not remembered them in the same way as their patriotic brothers. In fact, until very recently they have been virtually ignored.

The story of women revolutionaries in Kilmainham Gaol has almost passed from living memory. When I started this work there were four women who had been prisoners in Kilmainham Gaol: Nora Brosnan (b.1905), Maggie O'Toole-Rice (b.1908), Teresa O'Connell (b.1899) and Lily Thewlis (b.1898). Now only the latter two are living. All four women were prisoners during the Civil War. A large part of this book is based on interviews with these women and the descendants of their fellow prisoners, and on diaries, autograph-books, letters, and published and unpublished accounts of their experiences. It brings the ordinary members of the women's movement into focus and records the final days of Kilmainham Gaol as a prison.

Sinéad McCoole
1996

For Margaret
with best wishes
Sinéad
1998

9

Chapter One

THE NINETEENTH CENTURY BACKGROUND

*T*hroughout the nineteenth century, women's involvement in Irish political life and contribution to Irish nationalism remained largely unrecognised. Kilmainham Gaol housed many political prisoners since it opened in 1796, but Anne Devlin, arrested for her part in Robert Emmet's Rebellion of 1803, was the only female prisoner to gain renown in any way comparable with male patriots because her story was recorded and published after her death. Nevertheless, women always played a vital background and underground role in political and revolutionary organisations. They were, for example, crucial to the communications network of secret organisations like the United Irishmen in the 1790s, the Young Irelanders in the 1840s and the Fenians in the 1860s - carrying messages, providing safe houses and hiding weapons. On the whole, women did not attract the same level of suspicion as men, and remarkably few of them were arrested. However, in evading arrest they appear to have eluded the historical record, a fate which also appears to have befallen many of the women of the revolutionary period 1916-23.

THE LADIES LAND LEAGUE

The emergence of women as a recognisable political force coincided with the first moves towards women's liberation in the late 19th century. The pioneers were often women of exceptional or unusual background. The women who founded the first Irish women's political organisation, The Ladies Land League, were the

Fanny Parnell

sisters of Charles Stewart Parnell, leader of the Irish Parliamentary Party and the Land League. Fanny and Anna Parnell were the daughters of an American mother and independent spinsters who were both well educated and well-travelled.

The Ladies Land League, founded in America in January 1881 as a fund-raising organisation for poor relief in Ireland, was motivated by humanitarianism,

Anna Parnell

typical of an age when women expressed themselves through their philanthropic activities. The League only became politicised by necessity when Parnell and members of his party were arrested in November 1881 for opposition to the British Government's land policy. Anna Parnell led the women's wing of the organisation in a vigorous attempt to fill the vacuum left by the men's arrest. Membership grew rapidly to more than 5,000 members. The League was militant in its actions and many members were arrested (although none were sent to Kilmainham where the men were incarcerated). Parnell, who was anxious to move away from popular agitation to concentrate on constitutional attempts to gain Home Rule, suppressed the Ladies Land League shortly after his release in May 1882. The effect was to retard the development of women's political movements by almost twenty years.

WOMEN'S ORGANISATIONS, 1900-1916

Although women did join cultural movements like the Gaelic League (founded in 1893), they were excluded from political organisations. However they found an unlikely champion in a British soldier's daughter, Maud Gonne, who established Inghinidhe na hÉireann [Daughters of Erin] in 1900. The aims of Inghinidhe were the complete independence of Ireland, the popularisation of goods of Irish manufacture, the revival of the Irish language, and the restoration of Irish customs, games and dancing. Women's role as educators in the home translated into the public arena and contributed to a climate in which cultural nationalism flourished. Many who joined were young working women who discovered unprecedented freedom. In 1902 a drama group made up of Inghinidhe members called the 'The National Players' was founded.

Inghinidhe na hÉireann Group
(1905-1906).
The founder, Maud Gonne MacBride, can be seen holding a banner. It has not been possible to identify the other women. Their badge was based on the Tara Brooch.

They had their own newspaper, *Bean na hÉireann*, the first issue of which appeared in November 1908. At the time there was no other national paper of any kind. The newspaper sellers joked that it was *'the women's paper that men buy'*. The masthead for the first issue was designed by Countess Markievicz. Helena Molony worked on it 'almost without editorial assistance', but contributors included Arthur Griffith, Katharine Tynan, Roger Casement, George Russell (A.E), Countess Markievicz and Sidney Gifford (John Brennan). The paper ceased publication when the Irish Republican Brotherhood established *Irish Freedom* in 1911.

As part of its educational programme the group held lectures, among the more notable of which was one by the Countess entitled *'Women, Ideals and the Nation'*. Her conclusion was significant: *'And if in your day the call should come for your body to arm, do not shirk that either.'* [3]

In 1909, Countess Markievicz with Bulmer Hobson and Helena Molony, established a boy scout unit known as the Fianna. In 1911 girls were admitted but few joined. The handbook the Countess produced for the Fianna was considered to be the best training manual available. [4]

Ironically, the suffrage movement as originated in England was not supported by Inghinidhe na hÉireann, who objected to the vote being granted by 'a hostile parliament.' Arthur Griffith's Sinn Féin initially offered its support, provided women did not undermine nationalist objectives. When later the suffragettes did begin to do this, Sinn Féin withdrew its support. Individuals from the different nationalist organisations supported the franchise cause, but many felt that the issue should be addressed when Ireland had her own government. Hanna Sheehy Skeffington, who founded the Irish Women's Franchise League in 1908, believed that without the vote women would remain on the fringes of political life, and later viewed the formation of Cumann na mBan as a retrogressive step. In the aftermath of 1916 many old differences were swept aside. Women over the age of thirty eventually got the vote in the 1918 election, and Countess Markievicz was duly elected as the first woman MP to Westminster, uniting all factions in 'common sisterhood'.

The labour struggle attracted a large following of women, particularly in Dublin. When employers locked out union supporters in 1913, women workers who lost their jobs, like Rosie Hackett, an employee of the Jacob's biscuit factory, became politicised. Other women such as Helena Molony and Madeleine ffrench-Mullen joined the labour movement to give assistance, organising soup kitchens and the distribution of food for unemployed workers and their families. Many women also joined the Irish Citizen Army, formed in March 1914 for the protection of workers. James Connolly, one of its founders, ensured that women were treated equally in the movement.

By this stage other nationalist organisations were attracting women members. Arthur Griffith's Sinn Féin appointed Jennie Wyse-Power, who had been a member of the Ladies Land League, as its vice-president.

However nationalist politics was radically changed by the response to the third Home Rule Bill of 1912. When the Ulster Volunteers were formed in 1912 to resist it, nationalists countered by setting up the Irish Volunteers in November 1913. Cumann na mBan [The League of Women] was set up as part of the Irish Volunteer movement and amalgamated with Inghinidhe na hÉireann in May 1914 to become the main women's organisation in the country.

Members adopted a green uniform with a slouch hat. Their banner and badge carried the motif of a rifle with the initials of the organisation intertwined. An Inghinidhe branch was established, allowing members to retain a degree of autonomy. However, by virtue of their exclusion from the executive of the Volunteers, the women were subordinate in the movement, although the more militant ones protested that they were not *'the auxiliaries or the handmaidens or the camp-followers of the Volunteers'*. [5]

The aims of the organisation were to advance the cause of Irish liberty, to assist in the arming and equipping of a body of Irishmen for the defence of Ireland, and to raise money by organising céilís, concerts and other social events for the purchase of arms and ammunition. This collection was known as the 'Defence of Ireland' fund.

When the ratification of the Home Rule Bill was postponed until the end of the Great War which began in August 1914, Redmond called for the Volunteers to join the war effort in support of small nations. This caused a split in the Volunteers (those who supported Redmond were known as the National Volunteers). The Cumann na mBan Convention of November 1914 voted to support those Volunteers headed by Eoin MacNeill who opted to stay in Ireland, opposing Ireland's involvement in the War. As Redmond had the main support of the country, Cumann na mBan lost large numbers of members.

The Irish Republican Brotherhood (IRB) now began to use the Irish Volunteers as the platform to stage a rebellion. The absence of women members in the IRB (needless to say, an exclusively male 'brotherhood') meant that, like ordinary members of the Irish Volunteers, few women knew about the planning of the Rising that was to take place at Easter 1916 under the guise of routine Volunteer manoeuvres.

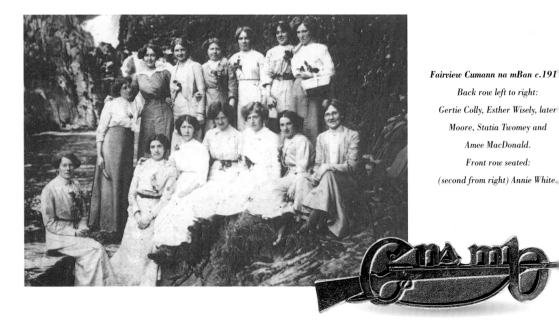

Fairview Cumann na mBan c.191
Back row left to right:
Gertie Colly, Esther Wisely, later
Moore, Statia Twomey and
Amee MacDonald.
Front row seated:
(second from right) Annie White.

Chapter Two

THE WOMEN OF THE RISING

*I*t is only very recently that the role of women in the 1916 Rising has been given significant attention. In the 1940s, R.M. Fox wrote an article 'How the Women Helped' which gave the impression that their participation was of secondary importance. Helena Molony, a member of the Irish Citizen Army, was frequently asked what role women played in the 1916 Rising:

I feel they might as well ask me what did the tall fair haired men do in the wars and what did small dark men do. My answer in both cases is the same: they did what came to their hands to do - day to day, and whatever they were capable of by aptitude or training. [6]

The exact number of women who took part in the 1916 Rising remains unclear, but it may have been as many as one hundred and fifty out of an estimated one thousand six hundred who took part. The main reason for the confusion is that the majority were not arrested. The official figure for those brought to Kilmainham Gaol was seventy-seven.

The women were members of Cumann na mBan, the Irish Citizen Army and girl scouts. There were also women who had no involvement in any organisation but seized the opportunity of getting involved. May Gibney was one:

On Easter Monday 1916 I volunteered for service at the GPO. I was not a member of the Republican organisation at the time but as a reference I mentioned the name of a Volunteer officer whom I knew would be on duty at one of the points ... I asked to be allowed remain at the GPO and was lucky enough to be accepted as a member of the garrison. [7]

One observer described them as women *'of all ranks, from titled ladies to shop assistants'* who *'worked on terms of easy equality, caring nothing apparently but for the success of the movement'.* [8]

May Gibney was a member of the GPO garrison in 1916 and was imprisoned in Kilmainham during the Civil War. She was engaged to Dick McKee, who was killed in Dublin Castle during the War of Independence. She is wearing the ring in which she kept a lock of his hair. Later she married Laurence O'Neill, Commander of the Carlow Brigade of the IRA.

The involvement of women in combat bemused observers who were at a loss to explain their presence. The *Weekly Irish Times*, a newspaper with a loyalist perspective, gave a colourful description of the women in the Headquarters at the General Post Office:

The girls serving in the dining-room at the Post Office were dressed in the finest clothes, and wore knives and pistols in their belts. They also wore white, green and orange sashes. [9]

Their role involved such activities as first-aid, commandeering supplies, cooking, and gathering information and carrying dispatches.

When Eoin MacNeill, Chief of Staff of the Irish Volunteers, discovered that a Rising was planned for Easter Sunday 1916, he cancelled the manoeuvres that were to signal the start of the fight. The Military Council planning the Rising was then obliged to send dispatch carriers around the country informing Volunteer units that the Rising would take place on the Monday instead. This task was largely given to women. Women could travel more freely than the men, but the danger of arrest was still high. Eily, sister of Michael O'Hanrahan, who was in her late teens, posed as an adult dressed in furs to deliver a dispatch to Enniscorthy. Julia Grenan was sent to Dundalk, and Mary Perolz to Cork, while others went to Tralee, Waterford and Borris. But because of MacNeill's countermanding order their efforts did little to over-ride the confusion, resulting in the Rising being largely confined to Dublin.

Julia Grenan

Dispatch carrying was even more hazardous during the days of the Rising, but women walked and cycled dauntlessly around the city, a target for snipers and arrest. One observer recorded, '*Cumann na mBan girls did practically all the dispatch carrying ... but none of them was unsuccessful. That was a point of honour with them - to succeed or be killed.*' [10] Chris Caffrey was one of the women arrested by the military. She was stripped and searched by British soldiers, but by that time she had already eaten the dispatch. When Catherine Byrne was sent by Pearse from Headquarters in the GPO to the Four Courts, he commented on her ingenuity when she rolled the note into her bun.

Neither did the women shirk leaving the garrisons *'under the deadliest fire to bring in wounded Volunteers'*. [11] A Red Cross nurse, attached to the British Army, wrote to a friend in England complimenting the women:

These Irish women, who did their work with a cool and reckless courage, unsurpassed by any man, were in the firing line from the first to the last day of the rebellion ... I never imagined that such an organisation of determined fighting women could exist in the British Isles. [12]

In the Irish Citizen Army women were treated equally as comrades in arms with the men. When James Connolly formed a women's section he made sure that the women shared in the same training and drudgery as the men. Countess Markievicz later remarked *'You may judge how fit we were when I tell you that sixteen miles was the length of the average route march.'* [13] In the weeks prior to the Rising (the Citizen Army had planned a rebellion of their own, until Connolly was co-opted onto the Military Council), some men in the Citizen Army complained that the women's section would be an encumbrance. Connolly threatened that if none of the men turned out the fight would go on with the women.

Helena Molony, stationed at City Hall during Easter Week, was equipped with her own revolver and ammunition. She had been taught to shoot by Countess Markievicz. During the Rising she was dressed in an Irish tweed costume with a Sam Browne belt. There is no question that she wished to be active in the firing line; as she later recounted, *'part of our military duty was to knit and darn, march and shoot, to obey orders in common with our brothers in arms.'* [14]

This view was shared by Margaret Skinnider, a twenty-three year old school teacher from Glasgow, and a private in the Irish Citizen Army. She joined the snipers on the roof of the College of Surgeons. In her memoir she wrote: *'It was dark there, full of smoke and the din of firing, but it was good to be in action ... More than once I saw the man I aimed at fall'.* [15] Not content with this activity, Margaret Skinnider insisted on being allowed go to bomb a house near St. Stephen's Green. She was wounded, shot in three places, but her only regret was to be disabled so early in the fight.

In Cumann na mBan the use of weapons varied from branch to branch. There had been classes in the use of weapons, but training in setting up a field hospital proved more popular. Winnie Carney, adjutant in the GPO, was armed with a Webley. In her Cumann in Belfast she achieved outstanding results in rifle practice. There were others in the GPO willing to use weapons. An observer later wrote *'Many of the women were snipers, both in the Post Office and in the Imperial Hotel'*. They were also on guard with rifles, relieving worn-out Volunteers. [16]

Unlike the Citizen Army, which assembled outside Liberty Hall before dispersing to their various positions, information regarding the change of plans and venues did not reach all the Cumann na mBan members. Many had no idea where to locate their Battalions on Easter Monday. Julia Grenan and Elizabeth O'Farrell, members of Inghinidhe branch of Cumann na mBan, became attached to the Citizen Army. *'We saw no objection to this,'* Julia Grenan related, *'because the Volunteers weren't taking any notice of us, didn't care whether we were there or not.'* [17]

Elizabeth O'Farrell

Éilís Ní Riain, a member of First Battalion Cumann na mBan, waited all day with a number of other women at their appointed location at Palmerston Place. The first indication they had that a rebellion was taking place was when they heard firing. *'At about 6pm we got orders which were brought by a dispatch-rider on a bicycle that we were to go home, as our service would not be required. We had no alternative but to obey the orders.'* [18]

At first members of Cumann na mBan were turned away from many posts, including the GPO. When this news filtered back to the leaders a directive was sent to accept any of the women who wished to take part. Only Eamon de Valera, Commander of the Third Battalion, refused to have them at his outpost at Boland's Bakery and Mill. He did not want women who were untrained for soldiering. Later he admitted that he was sorry that he had not used their help as some of his best men were engaged in cooking rather than fighting. However, years later he still maintained that women were *'at once the boldest and most unmanageable revolutionaries'*. [19]

The General Post Office

At first Winnie Carney was the only woman in the GPO, but throughout the next two days women continued to arrive and by the end of the week their number had risen to about forty. Catherine Byrne entered the GPO through a window on Prince's Street. She was immediately called on to tend Liam Clarke who had been injured when a home-made bomb accidentally exploded near him. There were no bandages to hand, so Catherine tore her petticoat and used it as one.

The women staffed a field hospital which was established at the rear of the building. The kitchen of the GPO was placed under the control of Desmond FitzGerald and Louise Gavan Duffy.

By Thursday it was clear that the GPO could not be held for much longer. Pearse gathered the women together and told them that without the inspiration of their courage the Volunteers could not have made their stand. They deserved, he said, a foremost place in the history of the nation. He then asked them to leave. At first they all refused, but finally a number of them were persuaded to go.

Even then many of them were reluctant to go home and reported to the Four Courts garrison. They were present for the final stages of the fight, and were arrested and brought to Kilmainham. Others, including Gertie Colly, made their way home but were held up by the military and detained for a short time at Broadstone Railway Station.

When fire broke out in the GPO on Friday 28 April it was decided that the remaining women should leave under the protection of the Red Cross flag. Some sixteen women, led by Louise Gavan Duffy, took the wounded to Jervis Street Hospital via passages broken through buildings in Moore Street. They sheltered in the hospital for the night. When they were making their way home the following day they had to pass their surrendering comrades. They evaded capture by saying that they were Red Cross nurses.

Three women remained in the GPO, Winnie Carney, Julia Grenan and Elizabeth O'Farrell. They stayed to nurse the wounded, including James Connolly, who had been shot while inspecting barricades. He later remarked to Julia Grenan and Elizabeth O'Farrell, *'When I was lying there in the lane I thought of how often you two went up and down there and nothing ever happened yez!'* [20]

By Saturday morning it was clear that the plan for the GPO garrison to join with that of the Four Courts would be impossible. The entire city was surrounded by troops. Aware of the loss of life among the civilian population, it was decided to surrender. While Elizabeth O'Farrell was chosen to deliver the surrender documents, Julia Grenan and Winnie Carney were arrested and taken with the men to the Rotunda gardens where they spent the night. The following day they were marched with their comrades to Richmond Barracks. Soon after they were transferred to Kilmainham Gaol.

WINNIE CARNEY (1887-1943) born in Bangor, Co. Down into a Catholic nationalist family. She joined the Gaelic League and was also involved in the suffrage movement. Her involvement in the Rising was due primarily to her friendship with James Connolly. In 1912 she became secretary to the Textile Workers' Union and a close confidant of Connolly's, who was then living in Belfast. A member of the Belfast Branch of Cumann na mBan, she joined the GPO garrison in 1916 as an adjutant and was responsible for typing Connolly's dispatches. She was arrested and held in Kilmainham, Mountjoy and Aylesbury jails until Christmas 1916. After her release her colleagues found her restless and uprooted. She took part in the Cumann na mBan convention in 1917, but her radical socialism alienated her from many of the members. Promoting a Worker's Republic, she stood unsuccessfully in the 1918 election as a Sinn Fein candidate. Her energies were afterwards focused on Labour and socialist activities, although she supported the anti-Treaty side in the Civil War. During this time she was arrested and held for 18 days and fined for possession of "seditious papers." She married George McBride in 1928. He was ten years her junior and a former member of the Ulster Volunteer Force who had taken part in The Great War. Her marriage to a Unionist led to her being shunned by both family and friends.

City Hall (Irish Citizen Army)

At 12.10 pm on Easter Monday a group of ten men and nine women of the Irish Citizen Army, led by Sean Connolly, marched on Dublin Castle. When they failed to take it, they took City Hall instead.

The City Hall garrison was soon supplemented by a group of women who had gathered at Christ Church Place awaiting instruction. When they were told of the outpost at City Hall they entered the building by climbing the railings and iron gates. Later Helena Molony and Molly O'Reilly went to the GPO looking for reinforcements, but the GPO garrison was unable to spare anyone.

Dr Kathleen Lynn, a Captain in the Irish Citizen Army, joined the City Hall garrison. Her first task was to tend to the fatally wounded Sean Connolly who died at 2pm, within hours of the Rising commencing.

City Hall was in a vulnerable position, and the rear of the building was shelled by troops from the Castle during the first night of occupation. Dr Lynn, the highest ranking officer following Connolly's death, offered to surrender. When asked if she was engaged in Red Cross work, she replied that she was '*a Red Cross doctor and a belligerent.*' At first the British did not know if they could accept capitulation from a woman, but in due course the insurgents were arrested. When the doctor was searched she was found to have an automatic revolver and fifty rounds of ammunition.

Dr. Kathleen Lynn and Madeleine ffrench-Mullen c.1916.

COUNTESS CONSTANCE DE MARKIEVICZ (1868-1927) was born into the Gore-Booth family of Lissadell, County Sligo. W.B. Yeats described them as 'a very pleasant, kindly, inflammable family.' [21] During her childhood, Constance was noted for her skill as a horse rider and showed ability in art. She was presented at Court and attended the London season for several years. In 1893 she began to study art at the Slade Art School, London and then in Paris from 1898.

In 1900 she married a penniless Polish count, Casimir Markievicz, a widower with a young son. They went to live in his home in the Ukraine for a time before coming to live in Ireland in 1903. They had a daughter, Maeve, born in 1901, who was given into the care of Lady Gore-Booth and brought up in Lissadell. However, the Markievicz marriage was not a success; the couple separated and Casimir left Dublin.

Thereafter, the Countess, as she was known, became increasingly interested in nationalism. She became a member of Inghinidhe na hÉireann in 1907, and contributed to its newspaper Bean na hÉireann. Together with Bulmer Hobson she founded a youth organisation for boys, the Fianna, in 1909.

During the Lock-Out of 1913, in which workers who supported the union were prevented from working, the Countess organised soup kitchens and joined the Irish Citizen Army,

The Countess in the uniform of the Irish Citizen Army (1914).

———

Background Image:
The Countess (Constance Gore-Booth as a child).

formed in order to protect the workers. During the 1916 Rising, as a member of the Citizen Army, she was Second-in-Command at St Stephen's Green. She was sentenced to death for her part in the Rising but her sentence was commuted to life imprisonment because she was a woman. She was sent to Aylesbury Jail and was held until June 1917. While in prison she was re-elected President of Cumann na mBan.

In the 1918 General Election she became the first woman elected to the House of Commons. She did not take her seat as she supported the Sinn Féin policy of abstentionism. She was made Minister for Labour in the First Dáil (1919-1921), but spent much of this period in prison.

The Countess opposed the Treaty and argued vehemently against its acceptance during the Dáil debates. During the Civil War she took part in the fighting, helped to edit the Republican newspaper Eire from Glasgow, and went on a fund-raising trip to America. Arrested again in 1923, she was held in the North Dublin Union.

Returned as an abstentionist TD for Dublin City South in the General Election of 1923, she refused to take the Oath of Allegiance and so did not enter the Dáil. The Countess joined the Fianna Fáil party at its foundation in 1926, giving up her position in Cumann na mBan to do so. She was elected to the Dáil in 1927 but did not have to swear allegiance to the King of England as she died on 15 July, before Fianna Fáil entered government.

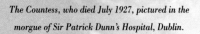

The Countess, who died July 1927, pictured in the morgue of Sir Patrick Dunn's Hospital, Dublin.

———

Background Image:
The Countess, her daughter Maeve and
stepson Stanislas c.1904.

NELLIE GIFFORD (1880-1971) Helen-Ruth, known as Nellie, was one of twelve children of Dublin solicitor Frederick Gifford. Nellie was the only one of the Giffords to take part in the Rising, although her sister Grace was engaged to Joseph Plunkett, and another sister, Muriel, was the wife of Thomas MacDonagh. Nellie was a founder member of the Irish Citizen Army. A domestic economy instructor, she gave lessons in "camp" or "emergency" cookery. As a member of the Stephen's Green garrison she was in charge of the kitchen in the College of Surgeons and delivering rations to the various outposts nearby. She was imprisoned in Kilmainham and Mountjoy for a few weeks after the Rising. After her release she went to England and eventually made her way to America. There she undertook a lecture tour on the 1916 Rising. She married in 1918 and had one daughter Maeve, born in 1920. In 1921 the family returned to Ireland. At the prompting of her daughter she organised a 1916 exhibition in the National Museum of Ireland during the Eucharistic Congress of 1932. It was mainly due to her efforts that a large number of items pertaining to the Rising were donated to the museum. She was also a founder member of the Kilmainham Jail Restoration Society.

St Stephen's Green and College of Surgeons

Michael Mallin departed Liberty Hall for St Stephen's Green with a detachment of Citizen Army members and began occupation at noon. Possession was also taken of the Royal College of Surgeons. Countess Markievicz arrived shortly after and took up her post as Second-in-Command.

Many of the women who were unable to locate their own scattered Battalions found their way to St Stephen's Green, among them Nora O'Daly, Bridget Murtagh and May Moore of the Fairview Branch of Cumann na mBan. Nora O'Daly was understandably apprehensive about their location:

The Green, even to a mind untrained in military matters, looked a regular death-trap, and although I was quite willing to die to help to free Ireland I saw no reason for doing so if I could help it before I had accomplished the purpose which had brought me hither, namely, to render all the assistance possible to the wounded and to save life wherever possible. [22]

Fifteen women under the command of Madeleine ffrench-Mullen, (who was later promoted to sergeant) commandeered vehicles, removed civilians from the Green, guarded the gates and tended the wounded. The first aid post was in the band-stand with the Red Cross flag flying to protect them. However the flag was of little benefit, and their white dresses with red crosses provided an easy target for the army marksmen. Amazingly, none of them were injured, although a bullet passed through one woman's skirt and another had the heel of her shoe shot off.

By Tuesday British soldiers occupied the Shelbourne Hotel and other buildings around the Green, forcing the insurgents to relocate to the Royal College of Surgeons on the west side. The women were arrested when Michael Mallin and Countess Markievicz surrendered on Sunday 30 April.

Marrowbone Lane

Eamonn Ceannt was in charge of the South Dublin Area with Headquarters at the South Dublin Union (now St James' Hospital). One of the outposts, at Marrowbone Lane, was the women's Headquarters, where they guarded the rear of the South Dublin Union.

There were twenty-one women in the garrison. Rose MacNamara was in command, with Marcella Cosgrave as Second-in-Command. During the week, apart from their first aid duties, the women appropriated a cow and her two calves and made bread and butter with the milk. Spirits soared after the garrison resisted an attack by five hundred British troops on Thursday. The women announced their intention of holding a victory céilí on the following Sunday. As it transpired, that was the night the garrison surrendered.

Marcella Cosgrave c.1916.

At the time of surrender the women could have evaded arrest, but Rose MacNamara went to a British Officer and informed him that the women were part of the garrison. They marched along with the men and were imprisoned in Kilmainham.

T H E C O O N E Y F A M I L Y . Twenty-year-old Annie Cooney and her younger sisters Lily (18) and Eileen (16) were part of Marrowbone Lane garrison during Easter Week. The Cooney family had a long tradition of nationalism. Their grandfather had taken part in the Fenian Rising in 1867. Annie joined Cumann na mBan in the summer of 1915. Her first job was selling souvenir booklets at the O'Donovan Rossa funeral. Through her work in Cumann na mBan she got to know Con Colbert (25) from Limerick, a member of the Fianna who was executed for his part in the Rising. Their brother Tommy was a member of the Fianna. Annie made her Cumann na mBan uniform the week before Easter, finishing it on Good Friday (now in the Kilmainham Gaol Collection). On Wednesday, Colbert and his men, including Denis O'Brien, whom Annie later married, joined the garrison at Marrowbone Lane. Annie, Lily and Eileen were among the twenty-one women arrested and brought to Kilmainham Gaol where they were held for the next ten days. On the Sunday the prisoners were allowed to attend Mass, where the Cooneys saw Colbert for the last time. Before he was executed he wrote to Annie and Lily sending his gloves and rosary beads as keepsakes. The sisters remained active in Cumann na mBan during subsequent years. Annie was one of the few women arrested during the War of Independence, and served four months in Mountjoy Jail in March 1921. Eileen tended the wounded in the Civil War when fighting took place in the centre of Dublin in July 1923.

Jacob's Factory

The Second Battalion under the command of Thomas MacDonagh assembled at St. Stephen's Green before taking over Jacob's factory in Bishop Street. When the women arrived they were told that no provision had been made for them. But Márie Nic Shiúbhlaigh persuaded MacDonagh to let herself and five others, Sara Kealy, Kathleen Lane, the two Pollard sisters, and Annie MacQuade, cook and take care of casualties. The only food that could be located was confectionery and they used what facilities were available in the factory.

When the time for surrender came Thomas MacDonagh called all the Volunteers together and told those who were not in uniform that they could leave. He was particularly concerned that the women would leave before surrender. Márie Nic Shiúbhlaigh later recalled:

I gave the girls MacDonagh's order. They did not want to leave. I could understand their feelings ... [MacDonagh] was anxious to have all girls out of the building before he surrendered. He feared that we would be arrested. If this had been the only consideration, I would have ignored his plea, and stayed; but he thought that the sight of the girls being arrested might upset the men - he wanted everything to go as quietly as possible. [23]

Four Courts

The First Battalion under Commandant Edward Daly established its Headquarters in the Four Courts. Daly only accepted women in the garrison when a directive came from Headquarters in the GPO. One of these was a young medical student from Longford, Bridget Lyons, a member of Cumann na mBan in Galway where she was studying. Her medical knowledge proved invaluable as there was fierce fighting with heavy casualties in the vicinity of the Four Courts. There were women also at the first aid station at Fr. Mathew Hall in Church Street. These managed to evade arrest, but those in the Four Courts were taken under guard to Kilmainham Gaol. [24]

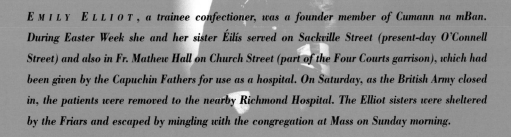

E M I L Y   E L L I O T , a trainee confectioner, was a founder member of Cumann na mBan. During Easter Week she and her sister Éilís served on Sackville Street (present-day O'Connell Street) and also in Fr. Mathew Hall on Church Street (part of the Four Courts garrison), which had been given by the Capuchin Fathers for use as a hospital. On Saturday, as the British Army closed in, the patients were removed to the nearby Richmond Hospital. The Elliot sisters were sheltered by the Friars and escaped by mingling with the congregation at Mass on Sunday morning.

Enniscorthy/Ashbourne

As a result of MacNeill's countermanding order few of the Battalions outside Dublin were active in Easter Week. However there was action at Enniscorthy, and the local Cumann na mBan under the command of Mary White took part in the fight. But the women were not arrested. The garrison at Ashbourne received word of the Rebellion going ahead from a Miss Adrian who cycled from Dublin with a message from Pearse. Miss Adrian, a middle-aged woman, made this journey several times during the week of the Rising and managed to evade arrest.

SURRENDER

One of the bravest women during the Rising was Elizabeth O'Farrell who carried the surrender documents to the different outposts on Saturday 29 April and Sunday the 30th. At 12.45pm on Saturday she left 15 Moore Street and approached the British Army post. An observer recalled, *'Inside her two companions watched her breathlessly, with lumps in their throats, afraid that every minute they would see the gallant little figure totter and fall. But as she advanced the fire slackened and finally stopped'.* [25]

At first she was thought to be a spy and had her red cross cut off her apron and sleeve. (The women involved on the Irish side in 1916 were not official members of the Red Cross, as the organisation could only be affiliated to a standing army, which was the British Army in Ireland). O'Farrell was held prisoner until 2.25pm when it was decided that she would be sent back to Pearse who would be asked to tender his unconditional surrender. She returned with Pearse at 3.30 pm.

Elizabeth O'Farrell

While her comrades from the GPO were surrendering, O'Farrell set out for the various outposts with the surrender documents from Pearse and Connolly. There were so many snipers in the area around Boland's Mill that she was accompanied by a British Officer, Captain Wheeler for only part of the journey.

So I started through the firing line from Butt Bridge to Boland's ... This was a very difficult job and I had to take my life in my hands several times. When I came into Westland Row the military were lined across the top and they were screaming at me to go back, but I kept on waving my white flag and the paper ... crossing Grand Canal Street Bridge the firing was terrific. At this point a man crossing the bridge about half a yard behind me was shot. [26]

By dusk that evening Elizabeth O'Farrell had completed her task without injury. After a short period of imprisonment she was released.

The hostility of Dubliners to the Rising was clearly evident when the garrisons surrendered. Immense damage had been done to the city and its normal functions were brought almost to a complete halt. Annie Cooney's memory of the journey to Kilmainham Gaol was of being taunted by the "separation women", who through the disruption caused by the Rebellion were deprived of the allowance paid by the British Army to the wives of men fighting in the Great War. They and their families faced hunger and hardship until the city began to function normally again. Years later Nora O'Daly recalled:

On Sunday to us came news of the surrender which had already taken place the previous days at some other posts ... We were marched ... men first, women following. I carried the Red Cross flag, as some extra-ordinary stories were afloat to account for the presence of women amongst the garrison ... On the way soldiers going the opposite direction frequently shouted, "Wot you goin' to do with this lot?" and the rejoinder was invariably "Ow, goin' to biyenet 'em like the rest." [27]

IMPRISONMENT

Kilmainham Gaol had ceased to function as a convict prison in 1910 and was taken over as an army detention barracks at the outbreak of the Great War. As the 1916 prisoners arrived at the gaol it appeared more forbidding than in its days as a convict prison. In particular, there was no lighting or heating because the gas supply had been cut by the Volunteers during the fighting. Nora O'Daly remembered 'arriving after dusk and being received by the light of candles, which only served to intensify the gloom, and did not prevent soldiers getting as close as possible to tell us many blood curling [sic] stories as they had time to repeat'. [28] The warders in Kilmainham Gaol were believed to have been military deserters. They were mainly curious about the Rising and asked what the women were 'in' for, and gave them gratuitous information about their own sentences and their sergeant's character.

The women were housed in the older west wing, built in the 1790s, which was in a state of disrepair with poor sanitary facilities. Annie Cooney remembered seeing an inscription which read "Sin no more lest worse shall come to thee." There were four prisoners to a cell. One blanket was issued to each. The daily routine began at 7am, although breakfast was not until 9.30am. Elizabeth O'Farrell described the dinner as *'awful stuff, neither soup nor stirabout'*. Served at noon, it consisted of stew and bread or potatoes. Prison biscuits were also provided. These served as makeshift spoons, as the prisoners had been denied proper utensils for security reasons. According to Nora O'Daly, the

Countess Markievicz being taken from Kilmainham to Mountjoy jail in May 1916.

biscuits were *'used as doorstops,'* and *'stood the wear and tear admirably.'* [29] Annie Cooney kept one of her 'Kilmainham' biscuits as a souvenir, and it still survives today!

The fact that many of the women knew each other and were able to share cells made their imprisonment a little easier. The British Military tolerated their camaraderie, but forbade Irish dancing at exercise hour on penalty of being kept in their cells. Countess Markievicz, who was held in solitary confinement, was not allowed to exercise with the other women.

Some of the women only realised that the Volunteer leaders were in Kilmainham when on 3 May they heard gun shots at dawn and suspected the worst. *'At first the warderess said it was distant fighting, but we knew the truth'*, recalled Julia Grenan. [30] Nora O'Daly was not aware of what was happening until the prisoners were told by the Military on Monday 8 May:

> *… we learned for the first time, with heavy heart, of the executions which had taken place, and this news sent my mind back to an occurrence during our detention and which had remained unexplained up to now. One morning we were awakened at the first grey dawn by a shot which appeared to be within the building.* [31]

Late on the evening of 8 May, when the women were preparing to go to bed, the cell doors were flung open, and they were ordered into the central hall. Those whose names were called out had to cross to one side and were informed that they were being released. As there was already a logistical nightmare with the vast numbers of men arrested, coupled with the fact that Britain was in the midst of a terrible war, the prisoners were released with a *'caution as to their future behaviour.'* In recommending their release General Maxwell clearly saw their sex as the decisive factor, writing *'In view of their sex ... I consider that it would be desirable that they should be granted their liberty'.* Nevertheless, twelve women who had been known to the police before the Rising were detained. General Maxwell was adamant that *'had they been male prisoners, I would at least have recommended for internment.'* He believed it would be unwise to have them *'at large'* in Ireland while such an *'unsettled state of affairs'* continued. It was decided to transport them to England under Defence of the Realm regulations. [32]

Among these prisoners were: Countess Markievicz and Brigid Foley, Citizen Army in St Stephen's Green; Mary Parolz, a member of the Citizen Army and Cumann na mBan, and the registered owner of the nationalist paper *The Spark*; She had been a dispatch carrier to Cork prior to the Rising; Annie Higgins, arrested on returning from delivering a dispatch to Co. Cavan; Helena Molony (Citizen Army, City Hall), who already had a police record having been arrested during a protest against the state visit of King George and Queen Mary to Ireland in 1911; Countess Plunkett, mother of Joseph Mary Plunkett, arrested on 9 May despite having played no part in the Rising; Kathleen Browne and Nellie Ryan, from Wexford, both from nationalist families and members of Cumann na mBan, arrested at Bray after the Rising; Madeleine ffrench-Mullen (head of the women's section of the Irish Citizen Army in St. Stephen's Green); Nellie Gifford (Citizen Army, St. Stephen's Green); Dr Kathleen Lynn (Citizen Army, City Hall); and Winnie Carney (Cumann na mBan, GPO).

These prisoners were kept at Kilmainham for about ten days and then moved to Mountjoy Jail in a Black Maria. During the first week of June, Mary Kate Ryan, Madeleine ffrench-Mullen, Kathleen Browne, Annie Higgins and Nellie Gifford were released. The remaining women were sent to England.

THE MARRIAGE OF
GRACE GIFFORD AND JOSEPH PLUNKETT

On 7 May, Lloyd's Weekly News carried the following account of an encounter between Mr. Stoker, a jeweller of Grafton Street, and 'a young and attractive lady, evidently of good social position.' who had entered his shop on Wednesday, 3 May and asked to be shown some wedding rings: ' ... despite her veil, it could plainly be seen that the lady's eyes were red with weeping, and she spoke with difficulty ... Surprised at her evident distress, Mr. Stoker gently inquired if she were in trouble. "You should not cry when you are going to be married," he observed. Then she revealed the whole tragedy, saying that she was Mr. Plunkett's fiancée, that he was to be shot the next morning, and that she was to be married to him that night. "For the moment I was thunderstruck," said Mr. Stoker, and didn't know what to say or do. Somehow or other I managed to express my sympathy with her terrible position, and she thanked me very quietly. Then she selected the most expensive of the rings, paid for it in notes, and left the shop.' [33]

Grace Gifford, sketched by
William Orpen (Private Collection). A study for
Orpen's painting "Young Ireland".

The young lady was Grace Gifford, an artist who had studied at the Slade School of Art in London. The daughter of a Dublin solicitor, Grace was brought up in the loyalist community of the Dublin suburb of Rathmines. But in spite of this upbringing Grace along with her sisters Sidney, Nellie and Muriel, became an ardent nationalist. Sidney wrote for the Inghinidhe newspaper Bean na hÉireann. She encouraged her sisters to accompany her on visits to Pearse's school St Enda's, where on one occasion Muriel was introduced to Thomas MacDonagh, a University lecturer and poet, whom she married in 1912. In time Grace met his friend, Joseph Plunkett, a poet and editor of a monthly literary magazine, The Irish Review. Joseph who was in his late twenties, was dying from tuberculosis and had to spend most of his winters abroad in the Mediterranean and North Africa trying to improve his health.

Background Image:
Grace Gifford Plunkett photographed by an American
journalist, October 1916 at Larkfield, Kimmage,
the Plunkett home.

By 1915 the couple had fallen in love and in December Joseph wrote to Grace asking her to marry him. On 7 April, 1916 Grace, a Protestant, was baptised a Catholic in anticipation of her marriage. The couple arranged to marry on Easter Sunday 23 April at Rathmines Chapel. However this plan was forestalled by the upheaval of the Rising which started the following day.

After being sentenced to death, Joseph sought permission to be married. Grace entered Kilmainham Gaol on 4 May at 6pm and was kept waiting there till about 11.30 pm. She did not see her fiancé until she entered the prison chapel, which was lighted only by a candle carried by a soldier. There were no friends in attendance, although her sister Nellie was a prisoner in the Gaol. The witness to the wedding was a soldier. Joe was hand-cuffed till he reached the altar and re-hand-cuffed immediately the ceremony was over. During the marriage they were not allowed to speak except to recite the words of the ceremony. Afterwards, Joe was taken back to his cell and Grace left the prison. At 2 o'clock she received a letter granting permission for her to visit her husband before his execution. She saw him in his cell for ten minutes. She later recalled: 'during this time the cell was packed with officers and a sergeant, who kept a watch in his hand and closed the interview by saying "Your ten minutes is (sic) now up" '. [34]

Grace's parents did not learn of the marriage until a few days later. Mrs Gifford told a reporter from Lloyd's Weekly News:

I did not know of my daughter's marriage to Mr. Plunkett until yesterday. I did not even know definitely that they had been engaged, although I had heard it stated. [their engagement was announced in Irish Life, 11 February 1916]. I did not ask Grace, and she did not tell me, because she knew I disapproved of the whole thing ... I first heard of her marriage yesterday from Grace herself. I went to see her sister, Mrs. MacDonagh, and while I was there she came into the room. She walked right across to me and held out her left hand, on the third finger of which was a wedding ring. I did not make any remark, but I knew she meant she was married. [35]

Background Image:

Posthumous sketch of Joseph Plunkett by Grace, June 1916. Used for the frontspiece of "The Poems of Joseph Mary Plunkett", (Dublin 1919).

Some of the women who were active in the Easter Rising, photographed in
the garden of Ely O'Carroll's house in Peter's Place, Dublin, during the summer of 1916.

Standing on the left:
A. Tobin, Aoife Taafe, Marcella Cosgrave, Mrs Kathleen Murphy, Bridget Foley.

Standing on the right:
M. Kelly, Máire Nic Shiúbhlaigh, Lily O'Brennan, Elizabeth O'Farrell, Nora O'Daly, Mary Murray.

Back Row:
M. Kelly, Brigid Brady, Jeannie Shanahan, Mrs Kathleen Barrett, Rosie Hackett, Margaret Ryan,
Brigid Davis, Chris Caffrey, Patricia Hoey.

5th Row:
Lucy Smith, Nora Foley, Pauline Morecombe, D. Sullivan, M. Elliott, Mary Sullivan, Tilley Simpson, Mrs Catherine Treston.

4th Row:
Nora Thornton, Rose Mulally, Shiela O'Hanlon, Maria Quigley, Margaret O'Flaherty, Josie McGowan, Eileen Cooney, Josie O'Keefe.

3rd Row:
M. Moore, K. Lane, Sarah Kealy, Gertie Colly, Mary O'Hanrahan, Amee Wisley. Bridget Murtagh, Cilla Quigley, Julia Grenan, Statia
Twomey, B. Walsh,

2nd Row:
Rose McNamara, Kathleen Kenny, M.J. Walsh, Mrs Lawless, Jenny Milner, Eileen Walsh, K. Kennedy, May Byrne, Annie Cooney,

Front Row:
Madeleine ffrench-Mullen, Miss Foley and Dr. Kathleen Lynn.

Chapter Three

WOMEN & THE ROAD TO INDEPENDENCE
1917-1921

AFTERMATH OF THE RISING (1916-1919)

*T*he work of Cumann na mBan in the aftermath of the Rising had a major effect in shaping the revolutionary spirit of the years 1917-21. The internment camps may have been styled the 'universities of revolution' but in Ireland it was the women who spread the doctrine of Republicanism throughout the country.

The women provided a communications system that brought together the disparate elements gathering under the umbrella of Sinn Féin in the months following the Rising. Women assisted the Volunteers by destroying papers and ammunition and delivering messages to the families of men who had been interned. Others searched for the dead and the injured in the hospitals - work that was vital in compiling a register of those widowed and orphaned or otherwise in need of support.

On the instructions of the Irish Republican Brotherhood, Kathleen, widow of Thomas Clarke, took a leading role in co-ordinating the relief operation following the Rising. Within a fortnight two organisations had been established, the Irish National Aid Association and the Volunteer Dependants Fund. Cumann na mBan encouraged and facilitated their amalgamation. The huge task of administrating the collection and distribution of money was undertaken mainly by Cumann na

KATHLEEN CLARKE née DALY (1878-1972) from Limerick. The niece of the Fenian John Daly. In 1901 she emigrated to America and married Tom Clarke, a Fenian who had been in prison with her uncle. They returned to Ireland in 1907 with their three sons. After 1916 and the execution of her husband Kathleen set up the Volunteer Dependants Fund. During the War of Independence she was incarcerated in Holloway Jail, became a District Justice and was elected to the Dáil. She opposed the Treaty. A senator from 1927-1936 and became the first female Lord Mayor of Dublin from 1939-1944. At the age of seventy-one she stood unsuccessfully for Clann na Poblachta.

mBan members. Seventy-eight Volunteers had lost their lives and the number of interned reached 2,300 at its height, affecting the means of some 10,000 persons. The organisation aimed to provide money for the welfare and education of the families of internees, as well as establishing employment for those victimised as a result of their involvement in the Rising.

Many of the women who had been involved in the Rising lost their jobs. Eileen Dempsey (GPO), who managed to avoid arrest, still lost her job at McCrad Collar Manufactures as a result of her membership of the Citizen Army and her involvement in the Rising. Éilís Ní Chorra, a member of Cumann na mBan in Belfast, never got the opportunity to join in the fight, but her sympathies were nevertheless known to her employers and who dismissed her for being absent without leave.

The Catholic Bulletin, *December 1916*
featured a series of articles and photographs
of the families of men killed in 1916.
The top image is of Áine (Fanny) and
Rónán Ceannt and the bottom picture is of
Muriel MacDonagh with her children
Donagh and Barbara.
Muriel drowned the following year.

In the Autumn of 1916 Countess Markievicz was re-elected President of Cumann na mBan while still in prison, and widows of the executed leaders were elected vice-presidents. The widows became a tangible symbol of the 1916 leaders' sacrifice, public figures giving a powerful focus to the highly emotional commem-orative masses that marked the first and subsequent anniversaries of the executions. The emotional effect of this public grief was reflected in a poem by Nora Ní Chatháin, entitled '*The Women of Easter Week*':

Honour the part they played
And their dedicated lives:
For great was the sacrifice they made
And the glory thereof shall never fade.
But greatest the price that was proudly paid
By the mothers of men and wives. [36]

For the commemoration of Easter 1917, the women were instrumental in the reflagging of the 1916 outposts. Helena Molony got a sailor to climb up on the GPO and hoist the tri-colour. The Proclamation was reprinted (copies are as rare as the Proclamation itself) and posted up around Dublin.

The recruiting drive begun by Cumann na mBan after the Rising was so successful that by 1917 two hundred branches had been set up. When the government attempted to introduce conscription to Ireland in 1918 women were prominent in the anti-conscription movement. Such an emotive issue attracted many women who otherwise would not have been politicised. On 9 June 1918 Cumann na mBan organised an 'An Ireland Women's Day' [Lá na mBan] as part of the campaign. Between 14,000 and 15,000 women signed the anti-conscription pledge at City Hall.

In the General Election of November 1918 Sinn Féin fielded candidates who advocated an abstentionist policy. Women took an active part in canvassing, propaganda and picketing at polling booths. Although Countess Markievicz and Winnie Carney were the only female candidates, the fact that women now had the vote must have had an affect on the successful outcome for Sinn Féin.

THE WAR OF INDEPENDENCE

The War of Independence (1919-1921) was never an officially declared war, and was in effect the first significant guerrilla war of modern times. The success of the underground war depended on widespread popular support. In this context the support of women, especially those who assisted the men in 'the flying columns' (of the Irish Republican Army), was crucial. Women provided safe houses and supplies, gathered intelligence, carried dispatches, provided medical attention (Cumann na mBan ran classes in first aid and drill), acted as look-outs, hid weapons, maintained records, and distributed propaganda.

*Ita O'Gorman, later **Draper**, with an unidentified Auxiliary*
who became 'very fond of her'. A member of Cumann na mBan
she used to gather intelligence from him.

*Catherine Wisely,
later O'Daly, a member of
Inghinidhe na hÉireann
and the Gaelic League.*

The difficulty of sustaining these activities was intensified when curfews and other restrictions (Cumann na mBan's main office was closed in 1919) were imposed. Cumann na mBan members befriended British soldiers as a means of gathering intelligence, a particularly precarious activity. They also continued to collect and distribute money for the dependants of Republican prisoners. In 1920 an American committee began fund-raising for the estimated 100,000 people who had been left homeless and destitute by the war. In January 1921 the White Cross was established in Ireland to distribute these funds.

When an underground government was established by Sinn Féin members elected in 1918, women worked for the departments and councils which were set up to challenge the ruling administration. Áine Ceannt and Áine Herron were among the women who took part in the Republican Courts, working as District Justices hearing petty cases. Others set up the Dáil Éireann Loan Clubs, selling Dáil Bonds door to door. The weekly door-to-door collections greatly increased their risk of arrest. Many of them were young mothers who collected and distributed material from their babies prams. They showed no compunction in using their children to allay suspicion. Catherine Wisely, a member of Inghinidhe na hÉireann and later Cumann na mBan, on one occasion carried twenty rounds of ammunition hidden in her baby son's clothes.

Thus despite the scope and nature of their activities, only as few as fifty women were arrested throughout the period. Sentences ranged from three days to ten years. Linda Kearns received a ten year sentence when her car was searched and 10 rifles, 4 revolvers, and 500 rounds of ammunition were discovered. Eithne Coyle, later President of Cumann na mBan, was sentenced to three years penal servitude for being in possession of a plan of the local RIC station and seditious material.

After two and a half years of war a Truce was declared in July 1921. By this time Cumann na mBan was affiliated to IRA Battalions around the country and had over 1,000 branches.

THE TREATY

The Treaty which resulted from negotiations with the British Government (October-December 1921) did not grant a Republic and required an Oath of Allegiance to the

British monarchy. Unable to accept this compromise, Cumann na mBan voted 419 to 63 against its ratification. It was the first organisation to declare against the Treaty and all the women deputies in the Dáil opposed its acceptance. *'The women of An Dáil are women of character, and they will vote for principle, not for expediency,'* declared Mrs O'Callaghan TD, widow of the Mayor of Limerick, Michael O'Callaghan, who had been shot by the Black and Tans. [37] Mary MacSwiney, sister of Terence, who had died on hunger-strike in Brixton Prison during the War of Independence, stated that if the Treaty was accepted she would be the Free State's *'first rebel,'* and that they would have *'the pleasure or the pain'* of imprisoning her as *'one of their first and most deliberate and irreconcilable rebels.'* Countess Markievicz echoed her: *'I am pledged as a rebel, an unconvertible rebel, because I am pledged to the one thing - a free and independent Republic.'* [38]

However, these formidable women were not representative of the opinions of the majority of Irishwomen, who wanted peace and supported the Provisional Government's stance, believing that the Treaty would be a stepping-stone to gain more freedom and eventually a Republic. The wives of men taking a pro-Treaty stance generally followed their husband's views. Among the prominent members to leave Cumann na mBan were Min Ryan, wife of Richard Mulcahy, who became Minister of Defence in the Provisional Government, and Mabel, wife of Desmond Fitzgerald, the Free State Minister for External Affairs. The broad popular support for the Treaty was reflected in a significant decline in the membership of Cumann na mBan, and the departure of moderate members meant that it became a more hard-line Republican organisation as Civil War loomed.

An Anti-Treaty group leaving the Dáil, after
refusing to take the Oath of Allegiance to the King of England.
The group includes Count Plunkett, Countess Markievicz, Cathal Brugha, Eamon de Valera,
Austin Stack and Erskine Childers.

The Civil War began with the shelling of Republican Headquarters in the Four Courts on 28 June 1922. The women had
shown how vital their role could be to the success of a guerrilla
campaign during the War of Independence. Now, however, the women on the
Republican side were well known to their former comrades on the pro-Treaty side
who were quick to appreciate the threat they represented. The mass arrest of
women supporters of the IRA from the outset of the Civil War must be seen as a
major factor contributing to the eventual defeat of the Republicans (or
'Irregulars') in the Civil War of 1922-23.

The women were more vulnerable to arrest than men on the run, and they
could be arrested and detained without charge under the terms of the Emergency
Powers Act. For the most part their offenses were comparatively minor: being
found in the possession of Republican literature, attending Cumann na mBan
meetings and collecting for the prisoners' dependants. The government however
was well aware of the importance of the women to the IRA's communications
network. W.T. Cosgrave, President of the Executive Council of the Irish Free
State, commented that *'the mainstay of the trouble we have had was the activity
of the women'*. When there were complaints in the press of 'a war on women'
Cosgrave countered that it was *'not possible to consider these women as ordinary
females'*. [39] Although the sentences for women were harsher during the Civil War
than during the War of Independence, the death penalty for carrying a gun was not

enforced on women. Seventeen-year-old May Zambra shot at a CID
(Central Intelligence Department) agent and Máire Comerford was
arrested in Loughlinstown with a revolver in her possession, but
neither was condemned to death.

Raids on the homes of well known Republicans became a
common occurrence during the Civil War. Áine, widow of Eamonn

---

May Zambra joined Cumann na mBan at sixteen and was imprisoned in Kilmainham Gaol the following year.
She was one of the youngest inmates to go on hungerstrike. She died in 1929 at the age of twenty-three.
She had been married to James Ryan, an ex-marine in the British navy and was five months pregnant.

Republican Woman's Jail Journal

MRS. MARGARET BUCKLEY, whose book, "The Jangle of Keys," is being published by James Duffy and Co. This will be the first woman's Jail Journal to be written in this country. Mrs. Buckley is a life-long Republican and was imprisoned in Mountjoy, North Dublin Union, and Kilmainham during 1922-23. She is an official of the Women Workers' Union, and President of Sinn Féin.

Margaret Buckley

Ceannt, who lived with her seventy-two-year-old mother, sister Lily and teenage son Rónán, was raided frequently. During a period of a month in 1923, the house was raided on three occasions and most of their possessions were destroyed. Margaret Buckley, later President of Sinn Féin, was arrested when her house was raided and Republican material was found. Sheila Hartnett was forced to move to Dublin when the family home and chemist shop in Kenmare, Co. Kerry, a suspected bomb factory, was burned down by Free State troops. She was one of the youngest interned in Kilmainham Gaol and in the North Dublin Union in 1923. Ciss and Jo Power from Tralee had been producing a Republican news-sheet entitled 'The Invincible' before they were arrested.

Many of those arrested were the mothers, sisters, daughters or girlfriends of Republican men who were imprisoned or on the run. One such prisoner was Annie Moore of Kildare. Her brother Brian, a labourer, was executed at the Curragh Camp on the 19 December 1922 for possession of arms and ammunition. On that day also her fiancé Patrick Nolan was executed. When Margaret Buckley met her in Mountjoy Gaol later that month she described her as an *'inconsolable looking girl'*.

Others arrested had simply been caught up in the struggle and had little interest in the fight for a Republic. Hannah O'Neill from the Liberties area of Dublin was arrested when detectives came looking for her son. When they could not find 'Sonny' they arrested her. She suffered greatly from arthritis during her incarceration. Her period of imprisonment did nothing to convert her to the Republican cause.

WOMEN PRISONERS IN KILMAINHAM
DURING THE CIVIL WAR

From November 1922 Republican women were arrested and incarcerated in prisons all over the country. The huge numbers being arrested created immense pressures on prison accommodation. By early 1923, over 13,000 Republican male and female prisoners were being detained. And so, having received its last female convict in 1881, Kilmainham Gaol was opened for the internment of female prisoners in early February 1923. During the eight months from February to November 1923 over three hundred women and girls aged between twelve and seventy were incarcerated in Kilmainham. They came from every part of Ireland, with especially large numbers from the Republican strongholds of Kerry, Cork and Dublin. A number of women who came from the Scottish and English branches of Cumann na mBan and the Irish Self-Determination League were deported, and others were arrested while transporting weapons between the two countries.

Ciss Power

The women were moved to Kilmainham after a protest at their detention with common convicts in Mountjoy. Lily O'Brennan, who had been one of the secretaries to the Treaty Delegation, was among the first group of women to arrive in Kilmainham on 6 February, 1923. As she and forty-two others were transported from Mountjoy in an open lorry they shouted 'Up Dev', 'Long Live the Republic' and other slogans. She

Jo Power

already knew Kilmainham Gaol, having been imprisoned there in 1916. But for others, like the Power sisters, who saw it for the first time in March 1923, it was a formidable place:

'When we got inside, ... the interior looked grim and forbidding and our spirits by now were sinking to 'zero' to be somewhat revived again by the strains of the hymn "Hail Glorious St. Patrick"' sung with great volume and devotion. We were marshalled along a stone passage and came to a big iron gate when the singing ceased and the prisoners came to the gates to discover who the latest arrivals were. Then pandemonium broke loose. Greetings were exchanged from those 'within' the gate and those without ... a good many of them being old friends and acquaintances from our native town.' [40]

Hanna O'Connor never forgot *'the edifice of gloom and misery,'* or the *'huge iron gates, the clang of the keys in the rusty locks, the dim gaslight.'* Brought into the east wing, she was struck by the size of the building in contrast to the comparative smallness of Tralee and Mountjoy jails. Here she was allocated her own cell, whereas previously in Tralee and Mountjoy all the 'Kerrys' were housed together in one room. The regional divisions were still maintained in the grouping of the women's cells. Though the new cells seemed bigger than their old ones, the windows left something to be desired; *'we missed the big windows of Mountjoy,'* wrote Hanna O'Connor, *'instead we had a small window high up, which left in very little light and which could not be opened.'* [41]

The East Wing of the Gaol, known as A Wing to the women. Concerts were held on the ground floor during the women's imprisonment in 1923.

The gaol was run by Free State Army officers and staffed by Free State soldiers and female warders who, according to Hanna O'Connor, were *'all well seasoned warriors'*. [42] One of the staff, a medical officer, Bridget Lyons, the only female recruited as a First Lieutenant in the Free State Army, had been a prisoner in Kilmainham in 1916. [43] O'Connor described the warder, Miss Dill, who to her dismay was said to be a fellow-Kerrywoman, as being *'as stiff as she could be, never smiled and never budged an inch to be helpful to us. Another specimen of the British type.'* [44] The staff were not all so unpleasant. In her book on her prison experience, *The Jangle of the Keys*, Margaret Buckley described one of the warders, a Miss Wilson, as kind and considerate.

The cells were small and basically furnished with a table, stool and a mattress on the floor. Those without gas in the cells got a large candle which had to last for two nights. But some luxuries were allowed. One clear if tacit recognition of the special status of the women prisoners in Kilmainham Gaol was that women convicts were brought from Mountjoy to Kilmainham to do the cooking and general cleaning. Margaret Buckley felt that they *'were glad to be there, as they had a much better time: tea instead of cocoa, less work and altogether freer conditions.'* [45] The Civil War prisoners were also able to take a bath each morning with warm water, provided by the convicts who worked the furnace. They were

KATHERINE 'JAKE' FOLAN was fifteen years old when she was arrested. The soldiers had come to arrest her older sister Mary who was not at home. But, rather than leave empty-handed, they took Katherine, who had been known to carry messages. She was initially imprisoned in Galway Gaol, but it proved embarrassing when the local papers carried reports saying that children were being arrested. The Governor of the prison was a cousin. In Kilmainham, 'Jake', as she became known, was housed in B wing in the cell that had been occupied by Patrick Pearse before his execution. In later years she recalled her period of imprisonment as one of the happiest times of her life.

also able to leave their cells. Fifteen-year-old Katherine (Jake) Folan's favourite past-time was to go into the padded cell in B wing and bounce about.

The convicts brought up the meals. Breakfast came at 8.30 am, dinner at 1 pm, and tea at 5 pm, and there was always something for supper. The only food that the Power sisters remembered was soup. This had to be fished out of a large container with tin mugs. It was served in a very unhygienic fashion, which they ignored when they were hungry. Some prisoners would not eat it and survived on the food parcels sent into them. Those who could afford it could have a standing order at the local shop for 'essentials' such as butter and cigarettes.

They devised an ingenious way of cooking in their cells. There was a gas jet in an aperture behind the cell door. It could be reached by placing a stool on top of the small table. By holding a can of water over the flame until it boiled, tea could be made. Food could be cooked using a large enamel plate. Nora Brosnan, a prisoner from Castlegregory in Kerry, thought it a wonder they were not all burnt to death. [46]

The prisoners were normally allowed to write letters and could receive any number, which was considered an essential concession reflecting their political status. It was the job of Peadar Kearney (composer of The Soldiers Song, now Ireland's national anthem) to censor all the post that came into the gaol. Hanna O'Connor recalled receiving a letter from a friend in which everything was cut out except *'Cheer Up Hanna it's all for Ireland - Mollie.'* [47] Not all the contents of the parcels arrived either. One inmate was deprived of her birthday cake, although the letter describing how it had been iced and decorated got through without editing. According to Margaret Buckley: *'The state of parcels depended upon the temper of the censor: if news from prison was published outside, a close search was made for a week or so'.* [48]

Parcels and letters could be halted without explanation. At one stage they were stopped for a three week period. Throughout the Civil War no prison visits were allowed. From November 1922 executions of men were frequent, and families feared for the lives of the women. The considerable strain this imposed on relatives is reflected in the stream of telegrams sent to the authorities in which they beg for news of the prisoners.

The Dublin prisoners were fortunate, as friends could come to the gaol. Inmates in Kilmainham were able to converse with those outside by shouting down from the third floor windows of the east wing, (see illustration below). Lily O'Brennan's cell was on the second landing. By climbing on the table, she could see the Dublin Mountains and people walking on the canal.

It was difficult for those outside to recognise people at a distance, but when the name of a prisoner was shouted a message was relayed and she would be brought to the window. There was usually quite an amount of competition to get the prime vantage points at the windows. Once there, they could spend hours chatting to friends and watching the world go by. Lily O'Brennan wrote in her diary that on Tuesday, 13 February she and another prisoner called Betty passed the time by reading advertisements on hoardings nearby. However when on one occasion an over-zealous sentry strafed the walls with rifle fire the activity had to be abandoned for a while.

'Communicating with Prisoners', (1923)
Jack B. Yeats.

Although the regime for these prisoners was more relaxed than for ordinary convicts, the members of Cumann na mBan imposed their own rules. Shortly after the arrival of prisoners, the highest ranking Cumann na mBan officers drew up a set of rules and these were read at a meeting on 23 February. A prisoners' council was formed and Commanding Officers were appointed. These were usually older women such as Mrs Ellen Humphreys, Mrs Margaret Buckley and Mrs Katherine Wilson. The tasks of the Quarter Master included the distribution of food, candles, soap and notepaper. An Adjutant was in charge of the collection and distribution of post. The highest ranking officers made representations to the Governor.

By March 1923 A wing (the east wing) was filled to capacity, and B wing (the older westerly section of the prison), was brought into use. Sanitary conditions here were poor and the building was in a bad state of repair. Margaret Buckley described her first impression: *'It smelled horribly; the cells were placed along narrow corridors, and all the passages were stone ... The lavatory was on the corridor, quite close to the cells, and as the weather became warmer, the air became foetid.'* [49] They were supplied with disinfectant, but when this had little effect they removed the glass from some of the windows. However, even though this made an improvement, as Margaret Buckley remarked, *'we paid for it later, when the wind blew in from the mountains, and we shivered under its lash'.* [50] The Governor was asked to replace the glass, but he refused, remarking that as it was they who took it out, it was they who could put it back.

The highest ranking Cumann na mBan members came from educated middle and upper class backgrounds. In a period when university education was open only to the privileged few, such women were well represented among the Civil War prisoners in Kilmainham. They organised classes according to the educational standards of the prisoners. Lessons ranged from the 'Three R's' to university matriculation standard. Intermediate French was taught. There was also Mrs Lavery's dancing class for those less interested in study. In keeping with the educational objectives of women's groups since the turn of the century, Irish language and culture was keenly promoted. Three nights a week, Dorothy Macardle gave Irish history lessons under the title 'Revolutionist History Class'. All the prisoners were encouraged to speak and read Irish. Many of the women converted to the Gaelic versions of their names. Lily O'Brennan was proud of her progress and wrote to her nephew Rónán, *'I am reading Irish well now - almost without a dictionary.'* [51]

Dorothy Macardle wrote short stories to pass the time during her period of imprisonment in Mountjoy and Kilmainham. A selection of these was published in

D O R O T H E A   M A C A R D L E (1889-1958) was the daughter of Sir Thomas Macardle, owner of the Dundalk Brewery Macardle, Moore & Co. Ltd. She was educated at Alexandra College, Dublin (1907-1911) and in 1914 obtained her Teacher's Diploma. She joined the staff of Alexandra as a lecturer in English. Even at this stage Dorothy had a very different outlook from other members of staff who were loyalists and unionists. ⁵² She encouraged her students to read and perform the writings of Yeats and Synge. During the War of Independence she lived in a flat in Maud Gonne MacBride's house and was secretly producing publicity for Sinn Féin. An ardent Republican during the Civil War, she was active both in the Women's Prisoners' Defence League and as a writer for the Republican newspaper Éire. She was arrested in November 1922 and held in Mountjoy, Kilmainham and the North Dublin Union. The Council of Alexandra terminated her employment because of her political activities, but she returned to the college after her release. A founder member of the Fianna Fáil Party, she served on the National Executive. From the early 1930s she was theatre critic for The Irish Press. *Encouraged by Eamon de Valera, she wrote* The Irish Republic *(Dublin, 1931) which for many years was a standard text book in Irish schools. She continued to write and one of her ghost stories* Uneasy Freehold *became a best seller both in England and America and was made into a film entitled* The Uninvited *in the 1940s. In the late 1940s she concerned herself with refugee children and her book* Children of Europe *(London, 1949) recounts the story of children in war-torn Europe. She was Vice-President and then President of the Irish Association of Civil Liberties (1949-1951). She never married.*

America in 1924 as *Earthbound*. Lillian Dalton Soiron, a former pupil of Macardle's from Alexandra College, supplied her with books and writing materials. She later recalled that in a letter in which Dorothy had asked her for a copy of Plato's Republic, the censor had crossed out the word 'Republic'.

Joseph Plunkett's widow Grace, an artist who made her living as a cartoonist, contented herself with drawing and painting on the walls of the gaol. One of her paintings, an image of the Madonna and Child, is preserved on the wall of the cell she occupied on the ground floor of the east wing.

KATHERINE GIFFORD WILSON (1875-1957) was the eldest of the Gifford sisters. She was a linguist and a graduate of the Royal University. In 1909, aged 30, she married Walter Harris Wilson, six years her junior. She went to live in Wales and only returned to Ireland when her husband died in the flu epidemic of 1918. Prior to the Treaty she worked for Michael Collins on the Republican Bonds scheme. She was arrested in place of Grace when the CID came looking for her. However, even when Grace was captured she was not released. After the Civil War, she was secretary to the Tailteann Games and was associated with the foundation of 2RN, the precursor of Raidio Éireann.

COMMEMORATING EASTER

On Easter Sunday 24 April, 1923 the women commemorated the seventh anniversary of the Rising. Lily O'Brennan wrote to her sister, *'it is like Easter week 1916 all over again here. The women I met for the first time then are in here now again.'* [53] May Gibney, May Gahan, and Nellie Ryan had been among the seventy-seven women prisoners of the Rising who were now serving sentences for their opposition to the Treaty. Among those related to the men who had been executed in this very place were Grace Plunkett, John MacBride's step-daughter Iseult, and James Connolly's daughter Nora. Áine (O'Rahilly) and Ellen (Humphreys), whose brother 'The O'Rahilly' had been killed in fighting near the GPO, were also prisoners.

At 3pm the 270 prisoners marched into the yard where the 1916 leaders had been executed. Hanna O'Connor described how *'a deep hush seemed to pervade the whole prison - gone was the buzz and the chatter.'* Grace Plunkett laid an olive wreath to their memory and Ellen Humphreys led the rosary in Irish. As Hanna O'Connor recalled it, there was *'no fanfare of trumpets - no bugle - instead the voices of hundreds of women prisoners, piercing the sky in recitation of the rosary in our mother tongue.'* [54] After

The programme of events for Easter 1923, from the collection of Hanna O'Connor, Kerry.

marching back to A wing, where the tri-colour was unfurled 'Faith of our Fathers' was sung and the Republican Oath was recited.

During the months the women were imprisoned in Kilmainham the death toll of those executed by the Free State Government rose. By the end of the Civil War seventy-seven had been executed. Cecilia Gallagher, who had only returned from her honeymoon when she and her husband were arrested, wrote of Frank, imprisoned in Gormanstown Camp: *'I am so grateful that he is still alive that I am content to abide indurance* (sic) *vile till it pleaseth the Lord to deliver us and give us once more to each other.'* [55] In April 1923, while Sheila Nagle was imprisoned in Kilmainham, she heard the news that her brother had been killed in fighting in Kerry.

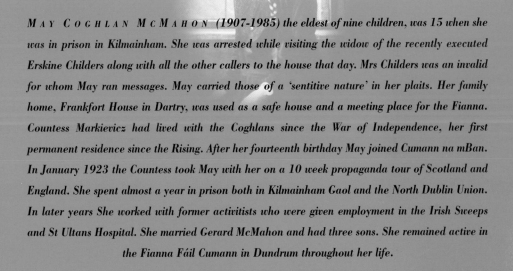

M A Y   C O G H L A N   M c M A H O N   (1907-1985) the eldest of nine children, was 15 when she was in prison in Kilmainham. She was arrested while visiting the widow of the recently executed Erskine Childers along with all the other callers to the house that day. Mrs Childers was an invalid for whom May ran messages. May carried those of a 'sentitive nature' in her plaits. Her family home, Frankfort House in Dartry, was used as a safe house and a meeting place for the Fianna. Countess Markievicz had lived with the Coghlans since the War of Independence, her first permanent residence since the Rising. After her fourteenth birthday May joined Cumann na mBan. In January 1923 the Countess took May with her on a 10 week propaganda tour of Scotland and England. She spent almost a year in prison both in Kilmainham Gaol and the North Dublin Union. In later years She worked with former activitists who were given employment in the Irish Sweeps and St Ultans Hospital. She married Gerard McMahon and had three sons. She remained active in the Fianna Fáil Cumann in Dundrum throughout her life.

Mollie Gill was employed as an artist with the Cuala Press, run by the Yeats family. She had been a member of Inghinidhe na hÉireann and later Cumann na mBan, for whom she organised meetings in Stepaside. She was 32 when she was arrested at her home on 9 March 1923 having been found in possession of a notice for a meeting of the Irish Republican Prisoners Dependents' Fund and a copy of the magazine Cumann na mBan.

ESCAPE TUNNEL

An escape plan was never far from the minds of the prisoners. In March, the occupants of B wing hatched a plan to break-out of Kilmainham. According to Margaret Buckley, *'the time-honoured idea of digging a tunnel took root, and though outwardly, the usual routine of educational and physical culture went on, time was also found for deeper delving.'* [56] The basement of the east wing, also known as the 'dungeons', was accessible from the main exercise yard. One of the rooms which had served as a laundry was the location chosen to begin digging.

It was an optimistic plan, given that Kilmainham's perimeter walls have foundations that go four meters below ground level. Although there had been several escapes from Kilmainham, they had always involved people getting out through doors and gates. A time-table was drawn up. Senior officers were not involved as their absence from exercises might have been noticed by the warders. The work was disguised by the din of the players of rounders and handball. Lookouts were posted, 'Kevin Barry' was sung to alert the approach of warders, and 'O'Donnell Abu' indicated that danger was averted. The first task was to remove a large flagstone about five inches thick. As there were no tools available the job had to be done with knives and spoons. The project added great excitement to the lives of the prisoners. When it was discovered by the matron after a month's work a long gaping hole four feet deep had been excavated. The diggers took the

Judy Gaughran

discovery stoically. Judy Gaughran laughed and May Connolly simply said 'better luck next time.' Sighle Humphreys wished to pass on the benefit of their efforts to future inmates, and wrote the location of the tunnel in pencil on her cell wall.

MARY MACSWINEY (1872-1942) born in England but was reared in Cork. At twenty she obtained admission to Cambridge University, normally reserved for men, and became a teacher. On her return to Cork she became an active nationalist. She joined the Gaelic League, Inghinidhe na hÉireann, the Munster Women's Franchise League, and Sinn Féin. She joined Cumann na mBan in 1914 and became a member of the Executive. She was arrested during the 1916 Rising and dismissed from her teaching post. Then she founded her own school, St Ita's. During the War of Independence her younger brother Terence died on hunger-strike. She campaigned in America, highlighting conditions in Ireland. She vehemently opposed the Treaty and went on hunger-strike during her periods of imprisonment. After the Civil War she defiantly advocated military opposition to the Free State. She died on 8 March 1942.

HUNGER STRIKES

The action of hunger strike was never adopted as a formal policy by the Republican leadership, but it came to be used frequently by prisoners during the Civil War to ensure that they were awarded political status and to hasten their release. The hunger strike was of course voluntary, but as the Power sisters recalled, *'It was amazing how quickly many of the prisoners suggested this deadly weapon as a means to redress grievances, and these were generally the ones who were on hunger strike before, and knew its full rigors.'* [57]

Mary, sister of Terence MacSwiney, who had died on hunger strike during the War of Independence, was the first woman to resort to a hunger strike during the Civil War. She began the strike immediately after her imprisonment in Mountjoy Jail on 4 November 1922. Cumann na mBan organised meetings and marched on the prison and government offices. A nightly vigil of the rosary was held at the prison gates. Free State troops fired shots over the heads of the protesters, primarily members of Cumann na mBan, and hosed and harassed them, which served only to enhance the publicity surrounding their protest.

On 21 November when Annie, the youngest of the MacSwiney family, was refused permission to see her sister, she encamped at the prison gates and went on hunger strike also. In protest at the exclusion of her sister, Mary MacSwiney then

A vigil outside Mountjoy jail, where the hungerstriking Mary MacSwiney was in prison. Her sister Annie and Mrs Despard are third and fourth on the left of the picture.

refused to have nurses or doctors attend her. On the twentieth day of her hunger strike her condition became critical. She was given the Last Rites. People from both Ireland and abroad lobbied the government for her release, and four days later she was set free. Henceforth, the strike was seen as an effective weapon against the Free State Government. Only a few days after Kilmainham admitted female prisoners, on 24 February, a strike was begun by Annie MacSwiney, now a prisoner herself. She was released after her fifteenth day of hunger strike. Ninety-seven women went on hunger strike for a week in March after all their privileges were denied without explanation on St Patrick's Day. Before that strike ended with the restoration of privileges on 22 March Nellie Ryan had started yet another one. She was the sister-in-law of the Defence Minister Richard Mulcahy, giving her strike great publicity value. She was soon joined by Kitty Costello and Annie O'Neill. Kitty Costello was 'a bad subject' for hunger strike and was suffering a great deal from the ninth day. Father Costello, Kitty's brother, wrote to President Cosgrave and appealed to him to have his sister released, reminding him that during the War of Independence their family had sheltered him and he had used Father Costello's clothes as a disguise. But the Civil War had already led to bitter strains and divisions in friendships and families, and Cosgrave refused.

By 11th April Nellie Ryan had endured twenty days of hunger strike, and Kitty Costello had completed sixteen days. Mary MacSwiney and Kate O'Callaghan had arrived the previous night and immediately joined the protest. The redoubtable Mary MacSwiney was not daunted by the prospect of another hunger strike of which she later wrote: *'the only kind of strike'* was when the striker realised *'fully the probability of death and [was] ready for it.'* [58] Maud Gonne MacBride, recently arrested for engaging *'in painting banners for seditious demonstrations and preparing anti-governing literature'* was brought to Kilmainham where she immediately joined the strike. [59] As these women were well known figures in Irish society their hunger strike had widespread propaganda value. Kate O'Callaghan was a TD and widow of the Mayor of